P9-BYU-833

COLLECTOR'S GUIDE TO

Feather Edge Ware

IDENTIFICATION & VALUES

Lisa S. McAllister

WWW.TINSIGNSUSA.COM
WWW.SDANTIQUE.COM
WWW.LEWISCLARKANTIQUES.COM

COLLECTOR BOOKS
A Division of Schroeder Publishing Co., Inc.

The current values in this book should be used only as a guide. They are not intended to set prices, which vary from one section of the country to another. Auction prices as well as dealer prices vary greatly and are affected by condition as well as demand. Neither the author nor the publisher assumes responsibility for any losses that might be incurred as a result of consulting this guide.

On the cover:
Clockwise from left:
Wedgwood rococo cobalt-edge pearlware coffee pot, $1,500.00 and up.
Large ironstone platter with blue edge, $150.00 – 250.00.
Rare brown shell-edge plate with brown Chinoiserie design and pumpkin slip band, $400.00 and up.
Covered milk pitcher in the Mared pattern, $950.00 and up.
Mug with embossed green edge, $350.00 – 450.00.
Pearlware green-edge sauce tureen, $400.00 – 500.00.

Cover design by Beth Summers
Book design by Joyce Cherry

Searching for a Publisher?

We are always looking for knowledgeable people considered to be experts within their fields. If you feel that there is a real need for a book on your collectible subject and have a large comprehensive collection, contact Collector Books.

Collector Books
P. O. Box 3009
Paducah, KY 42002-3009
www.collectorbooks.com

Copyright © 2001 by Lisa McAllister

All rights reserved. No part of this book may be reproduced, stored in any retrieval system, or transmitted in any form, or by any means including but not limited to electronic, mechanical, photocopy, recording, or otherwise, without the written consent of the author and publisher.

Contents

Acknowledgments

Thanks to the following businesses and individuals for their help:
Firstlook Photo, Hagerstown, MD, and Virginia Barnes
Dayna Harple
Rodney Harmic

All photography by Lisa S. McAllister

Items from the collections of:
Patrick Dooley
Glenna Fitzgerald
Ed Goodhart
Gene Haney
Barry and Lisa McAllister
Dennis and Patricia Schultz
Wayne and Rosemary VanDerzell
Karen Wendheiser

Many thanks to all the collectors who loaned their pieces for inclusion in this book. Thanks, too, for your help in the photography process. It is a lot of work carrying pieces back and forth, and being very careful all the while not to trip over your dog or cat or parrot. I could not have done this book without your help.

Thanks to Barry McAllister, who must wonder sometimes when he pays the bills, what does she do with all that film? Thank you for your encouragement and the time needed to write.

This book would also not have been possible without the assistance of Gene Haney. He is a generous and educated man whom I have had the luck to know. I thank you, Gene, for sharing your knowledge with all of us.

Lisa S. McAllister

There is no better way to invite criticism than to write a book! There is always someone who knows more than you do, or has a photo of "something that is not in your book."

This book is intended to be a primer on feather edge ware. It is a general explanation of body types, makers, and the colors and forms produced. The variety of forms shown is in no way all-encompassing, with new examples surfacing all the time.

The earliest examples of shell edge decoration have a feathered design around the rim. This feathering may have contributed to the misnomer of feather edge when actually referring to shell edge. The molded feather edge of creamware was very rarely decorated. In contrast, the incised or molded borders of pearlware and later whiteware bodies were always colored. These molded borders compounded the already confused names of the two distinctly different border designs. I was at a loss for a general name to give this ware. After much deliberation, I decided on feather edge. The different edges are explained in this guide, so the reader will be able to discern shell edge from embossed edge, but the name feather edge is a fully applicable, though not technically correct, term. There is no intent to confuse or mis-educate the reader. It is a much better term than "Leeds," a name that applies only to wares made at the Leeds Pottery! Also, most people who enjoy this pottery already call it feather edge. A more correct way to define feather edge would be to call it blue-edge, green-edge, etc., but I am not out to change the world.

Feather edge was produced in England (with a few Continental and American examples extant). It was used all over the world, but pottery-hungry Americans were the largest consumers. Enoch Wood shipped 262,000 pieces of feather edge in a single consignment. Feather edge was cheap but used by people of every economic and social strata. Prices continued to drop after the Industrial Revolution as goods were less expensive to produce; feather edge now had much more competition from decorated wares as well. It was sold mostly as dinner services. The following is a representative service taken from Josiah Wedgwood's first Queen's ware catalog in 1774. (Generally, the same vessels continued to be produced into the nineteenth century, although some shapes will vary.) Keep in mind, this service was considered of "middling" size:

2 oval dishes, 19 inches	2 terrines for soup
2 oval dishes, 17 inches	2 sauce terrines
2 round dishes, 17 inches	4 sauce boats
2 round dishes, 15 inches (Most of these "dishes" are platters.)	2 salad dishes
	6 salts
4 oval dishes, 15 inches	2 mustard pots
4 oval dishes, 13 inches	4 pickle dishes
4 oval dishes, 11 inches	6 dozen flat plates
4 round dishes, 11 inches	2 dozen soup plates
4 covered dishes	

That's 146 pieces, in case you weren't counting, and as many as 96 of them could be plates and platters!

The condition of the pieces you buy is a personal choice. However, the more rare a piece of feather edge, the more damage and/or repair is acceptable. It is a good idea to own at least a few restored pieces, to educate yourself. Many of the pieces shown in this book are 200 years old. Trying to build a collection, all in perfect condition, shouldn't even be a consideration.

A Discussion of Pottery Bodies

Earthenware was the body used for feather edge ware. A simplified chronology of earthenware follows.

TIN-GLAZED OR DELFTWARE: c. 1400 – c. 1750

A buff earthenware, fired at 1,000 degrees, then covered with a water-based glaze containing tin oxide. When dry, the surface was white and powdery. Decorated at this point with color (polychrome and/or blue). Fired again at 1,000 degrees.

Identification: Glassy white glaze, sometimes pitted. Bright, enamel underglaze decoration. Easily chipped or flaked surface.

WHITE SALT-GLAZED STONEWARE: c. 1720 – c. 1750

Stoneware, composed of clay and flint, which is covered by a salt glaze. During the hottest point of firing, salt was thrown into the kiln. The high heat (1,200 degrees to 1,350 degrees) split the salt into its basic components of sodium and chlorine. The chlorine was vented through the chimney as the sodium combined with the silica of the applied glaze.

Identification: Surface appears to be pitted and may be compared to that of an orange peel. Pale gray or off-white in color. Hard but delicate body exhibiting fine workmanship.

CREAMWARE: c. 1750 – c. 1780

Earthenware made with the same materials as stoneware but fired at a lower temperature (900 to 1,100 degrees) and lead glazed before firing. Much of the creamware produced at this time was made by potters producing salt-glazed stoneware, so the same forms can be found using both wares. Around 1740 to 1750, an important process was developed, allowing for a first, or biscuit, firing prior to glazing. The glaze also was changed from a powder to a liquid, incorporating flint and lead ground in water. It was applied prior to the second firing.

The gradual development of creamware in the eighteenth century was considered most important. There was much competition at the time to refine it. The first creamware produced was not the creamware we think of today. It was heavier and darker, with glazes in yellow, brown or blue. In the 1750s and 1760s a few potters, notably Wedgwood, were producing a dramatically refined creamware body, due to the introduction of china clay and china stone. This was used in both the body and the glaze. This new body was much paler and lighter in weight than the first creamware. Dubbed "Queen's ware" by Wedgwood, more potters were producing the lighter ware by the 1770s, but both darker and lighter pieces were made in the same time period. Creamware was produced in very large quantities and was used the world over.

This is the first body to which feather edge was applied. Typically seen feather edge decorated creamware was produced by Wedgwood, although other potters are known to have made it at this time as well, such as Leeds, Herculaneum, and Neale & Co. Very little decorated edge creamware was produced in total, however.

Identification: Buff to pale yellow colored earthenware with fine details on a thin, lightweight body. Puddled glaze will appear yellow or yellow-green.

PEARLWARE: c. 1780 – c. 1830

A very white bodied earthenware due to the use of a glaze containing cobalt. Also a factor in the stark whiteness of the body was the larger proportion of china clay and flint added to the existing creamware body. A variety of glazes were used, including alkalines and lead.

Pearlware was introduced by Josiah Wedgwood in 1779. He was looking for something new to offer the fickle public, but even he did not take pearlware seriously. He thought of it as an addition, not a replacement, and so underrated the demand of the public; the length of production was nearly double that of creamware. Pearlware was developed to compete with porcelain, hence the bright white body, and the name "pearl white." Pearlware was also referred to as "Blue and White Ware," probably due to the fact that when it was first in use in America, in the late 1780s and 1790s, much of it was transfer printed in underglaze blue. Pearlware became a bridge between the saturation of creamware and the production of later earthen bodies.

Much of the feather edge found today is on a pearlware body, due to at least 50 years of production.

Identification: Both body and glaze appear a bright white color. Harder body due to increased flint in the clay. Puddled glaze will appear blue or greenish blue. In some examples, identical forms as creamware. Heavier than creamware but still light in weight.

WHITEWARE/STONEWARE: c.1805 –

Earthenware, forming a dense white body, which is thicker and heavier than either pearlware or creamware. This body was obtained by the addition of even more flint and china clay, and also adding oxide of cobalt as a further whitening agent. A variety of glazes were used, mainly consisting of feldspar and borax. Lead glazes were discontinued on this ware.

Whiteware, and the later ironstone, were developed for use as a cheap and sturdy tableware. Since their target was the average working man, it is easy to ascertain the distribution of wealth in our country at its time of production, by the amount of these products found. The quality of Chinese imports worked as a catalyst to spur English potters into producing better whitewares.

Wedgwood developed whiteware in 1805, and Mason patented the process of producing ironstone in 1813. Presently, the two terms are considered interchangeable.

Quite a bit of whiteware and ironstone were produced bearing a feathered edge, due to an almost 80-year span of production.

Identification: Hard, sometimes thick body, heavier in weight. Glossy. Often marked.

Types of Manufacture

BAT MOLDING: A "bat" or disc of clay was pressed into a mold. Best used for thicker plates and bowls.

DRAPE MOLDING: A flat piece of clay was draped over a mold made of either plaster, wood or clay and allowed to dry before removal. Plates and similar forms were produced by drape molding.

CASTING: Casting or slip casting involved pouring slip (liquid clay) into a plaster mold (of one or more pieces) and removing the object once the clay was dry. This could be used to produce bodies, handles, spouts, knobs, etc.

PRESS MOLDING: Press molding involved pressing or forcing the clay into or onto a mold, or onto a block, and removing when the clay was dry. Used for producing bodies, spouts, handles, knobs, etc.

These are eighteenth and nineteenth century press-molded finials.

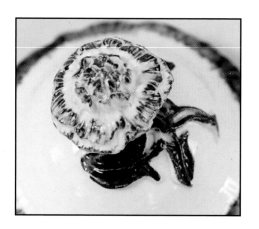

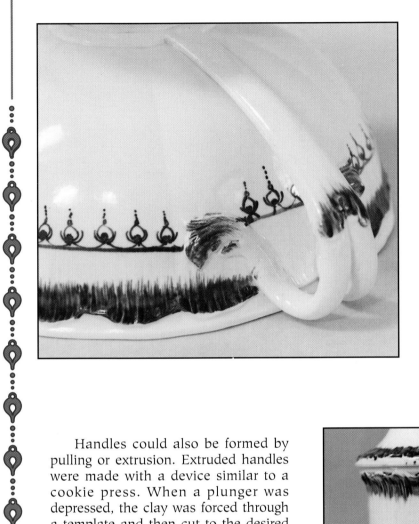

Molded handle on Wedgwood Mared round tureen, c.1775 – 1790.

Handles could also be formed by pulling or extrusion. Extruded handles were made with a device similar to a cookie press. When a plunger was depressed, the clay was forced through a template and then cut to the desired length.

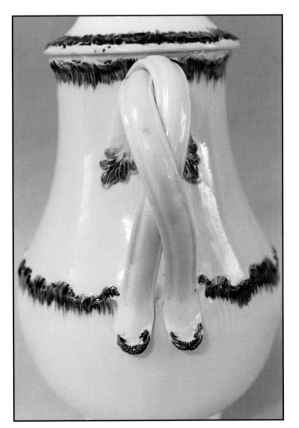

Extruded (twined) handle, Wedgwood coffee pot, c. 1775 – 1790.

A general idea of age may be ascertained by the care with which the border color is applied. From the meticulously applied and brushed feathering of the earliest examples, it is easy to chart the progression (and decline) of the edge decoration and type of earthenware body used.

Feather edge forms appeared in both salt-glaze and creamware c. 1765. Their rims were never decorated as the later shell-edge rims were.

Shell edge designs provided the most popular colored edge earthenware and was used by potters from at least 1755. The shell was a much-used motif on other types of ceramics as well as furniture of the period. Wedgwood's shell-edge design became the standard for the industry. Forms were either creamware or pearlware.

The first pattern book of Wedgwood, compiled c. 1770, includes the following shell edge designs:

No. 7 Blue shell edge
No. 8 Blue shell edge, scroll on verge (also known as Mared or Wedgwood Onion)
No. 83 Green shell edge, underglaze
No. 175 Red-brown shell edge

By 1818 imports of both blue and green edged pearlware surpassed that of creamware. This trend, which began after the War of 1812, made all types of edged wares financially available to the general public. Embossed edges predominate.

After 1840, whiteware gradually replaced pearlware as a major import. It was cheaper and sturdier than pearlware. The attention to edge decoration declined to the point of being nominal.

Regardless of body, blue was the most common and popular edge color. Green was second, followed by all other edge colors.

Progression of Edges

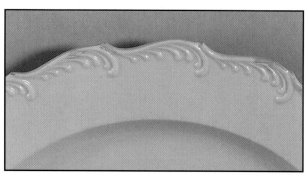

1. Feather edge – Evenly scalloped rim with embossed feather design. Creamware or salt glaze body. Edge never colored. C.1750 – 1800.

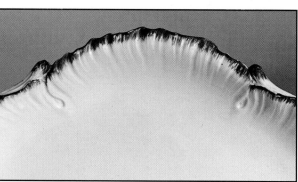

2. Asymmetrical (uneven) – Scalloped edge with impressed shell design. Edges cut by hand. Rococo edges also come under this category. Edge color underglaze or overglaze with fine feathering. C.1775 – 1820. Edge colors: Blue, green, aqua, black, mulberry, red, yellow, brown.

3. Shell rim with even scallop and impressed design – Finely cut molded edge and feather-painting. C.1780 – 1820. Edge colors: Blue, green, yellow, red, brown, gilded, aqua.

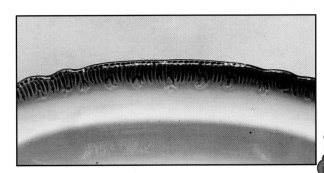

4. Embossed edge (with additional rim embossing) – Designs seen are agrarian motifs such as grapes and wheat, fish scales, and nonrepresentational geometric motifs. Edge color is usually confined to a wide painted band. C.1820 – 1830. Edge colors: Blue, green, red, yellow.

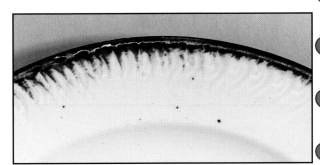

5. Plain rim with impressed design, c.1830 – 1860. Impressed design usually confined to plain, incised-looking edge; edge color is a thin band. Edge colors: Blue, green, red.

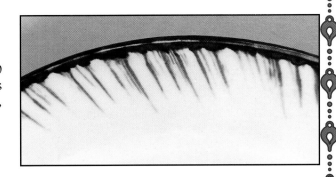

6. Plain rim without impressed design, c.1860 – 1890. Edge color usually a band; at times quite heavily feathered. Edge colors: Blue, green, red.

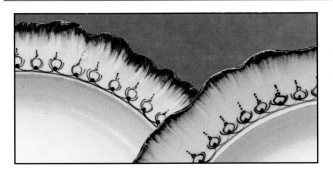

An example of the difference between Asymmetrical and Rococo edges. Asymmetrical, with "knot" or "eye" on left; Rococo, without "knot" or "eye" on right. Both are hand-cut edges; these pieces were made by Wedgwood.

TRANSFER PRINTING: Transfer printing was first used about 1775. A copper plate was engraved with a design. Color was rubbed into the lines of the warmed plate and the excess paint removed. Moistened tissue paper was placed over the plate and pressed onto the plate. Then the paper was removed from the metal plate and pressed onto the earthenware piece. The paper was rubbed to transfer the design, and the earthenware was put into water to remove the paper.

Transfers on feather edge could be over or under the glaze. There were a variety of transfers used: genre (scenes of everyday life); children; animals or birds; historical (Lafayette was a popular transfer used on feather edge plates); neoclassical or mythological. Some transfers had verses, usually children's plates. Monograms or crests were used when a set of feather edge was ordered. Most transfers were done in blue because the color would hold up to the high temperatures in the kiln. Other colors, such as green, black, and mulberry, were also used, but the source of their color was harder to obtain than cobalt.

Transfer printing was also done with a bat in the late eighteenth century. The bat used in transfer printing was a disc of gelatine or soft glue and was used instead of paper.

Transfer-painted children's plate.

FREEHAND PAINTING: The sky was the limit for designs that were painted by hand. While transfers tended to be copied from existing prints, hand painting was at the discretion of the painter. That being said, he or she still had to follow the trends of the day. Flowers were the most used subject, although fruit and birds were popular, too. Freehand painting could be under or over the glaze. The design was stencilled on in charcoal after the first firing, before being painted onto the piece.

Blue looked so good on the stark whiteness of pearlware that it was a major incentive for competing with Chinese porcelains. A design that was quite in demand in the late eighteenth century was the willow-type motif in underglaze blue, referred to as Chinoiserie. It was a European copy of a Chinese design. The four main elements in the Chinoiserie design are a house, a fence, birds, and an androgynous figure referred to as Long Eliza. Most examples will contain the house, fence, and birds. The best possible example of Chinoiserie would also contain the figure. See an example on page 38.

Polychrome painting, i.e., two or more colors, could be in Pratt-type colors or enamel colors. Pratt colors are yellow, orange, green, blue, brown, black, and a brownish-purple. This is another occasion where the dreaded "Leeds" pops up again as a misnomer, probably because Leeds was one of the makers of polychrome-decorated feather edge. Enamel colors were more varied and brighter, stronger: black, red, chrome yellow, etc. Also, Pratt-type colors tended to be underglaze, while enamel colors were usually done after the last firing. A plate showing this type of decoratin is shown on page 37.

Although there were hundreds of potteries producing creamware, pearlware, and whiteware, these are the most recognizable manufacturers of feather edge. Not all marks of each pottery are listed, only the most frequently seen marks pertaining to feather edge. Note that, generally, earlier marks are impressed, later marks are stamped. In the late 1880s the McKinley Tariff Act was passed. Beginning in 1891 every mark had to include "ENGLAND." After 1901, the same act required the wording to change to "MADE IN ENGLAND."

STAFFORDSHIRE

Manufacturers	Dates	Marks
William Adams & Sons, Ltd.	c.1769 – c.1900	ADAMS & CO., 1769 – 1800, impressed; ADAMS WARRANTED STAFFORDSHIRE, 1804 – 1840, in a circle with eagle; the same but with crown, 1810 – 1825, both impressed; WM. ADAMS & CO. TUNSTALL ENGLAND, 1879 – c.1900, eagle & registry mark; black ink stamp
James & Ralph Clews	c.1818 – c.1834	CLEWS WARRANTED STAFFORDSHIRE; impressed in a circle, with crown
Copeland & Garrett	c.1833 – c.1847	COPELAND & GARRETT; printed
Davenport	c.1793 – c.1820	Davenport, DAVENPORT, with or without anchor, impressed
William Greatbatch	c.1760 – c.1780	GREATBATCH; impressed
John & Ralph Hall	c.1802 – c.1822 c.1811 – c.1822	HALL, impressed
J. Heath	c.1780 – c.1800	I.H., HEATH; impressed
J & G Meakin (Ltd.)	c.1851 –	J & G MEAKIN; impressed or printed
John Meir & Son	c.1890 – c.1900	IRONSTONE JOHN MEIR & SON ENGLAND; black ink stamp with crown, unicorn, and lion
(James) Neale & Co.	c.1776 – c.1786	NEALE & CO.; impressed

Powell & Bishop	c.1876 – c.1878	POWELL & BISHOP; in oval cartouche, impressed
John & George Rogers	c.1784 – c.1814	ROGERS; impressed
John Rogers & Son (Spencer)	c.1814 – c.1836	ROGERS; impressed
Shorthose and Heath	c.1795 – c.1815	SHORTHOSE & HEATH, possibly Shorthose & Co.; impressed or printed
Smith Child	c.1780 – c.1790	CHILD; impressed
Andrew Stevenson	c.1816 – c.1830	STEVENSON, with ship in elliptical cartouche, A. STEVENSON WARRANTED STAFFORDSHIRE, in a circle with crown; both marks impressed
Joseph Stubbs	c.1822 – c.1835	STUBBS; impressed
Stubbs & Kent	c.1828 – c.1830	STUBBS & KENT LONGPORT; impressed or printed in a circle
John Turner	c.1762 – c.1806	TURNER; impressed
Josiah Wedgwood	c.1759 – c.1860	WEDGWOOD; impressed
Enoch Wood	c.1784 – c.1790 (92)	WOOD, E. WOOD, E. W., W, W(***); impressed
Enoch Wood & Sons	1818 – 1846	ENOCH WOOD & SONS BURSLEM; with or without eagle; impressed
Wood & Caldwell	c.1790 (92) – July 1818	WOOD & CALDWELL; impressed
Ralph Wood	c.1781 – c.1801	R. WOOD; impressed or incised

YORKSHIRE

Don Pottery	c.1801 – c.1830	DON POTTERY; impressed
Ferrybridge	c.1804+	FERRYBRIDGE; impressed
Leeds, Hartley, Greens & Co.	c.1760 – c.1800+	LEEDS POTTERY; impressed

LIVERPOOL

Fell	c.1817 – c.1830	FELL; impressed
Herculaneum	c.1796 – c.1833	HERCULANEUM; impressed

MAJOR POTTERY CENTERS

OF

ENGLAND AND WALES

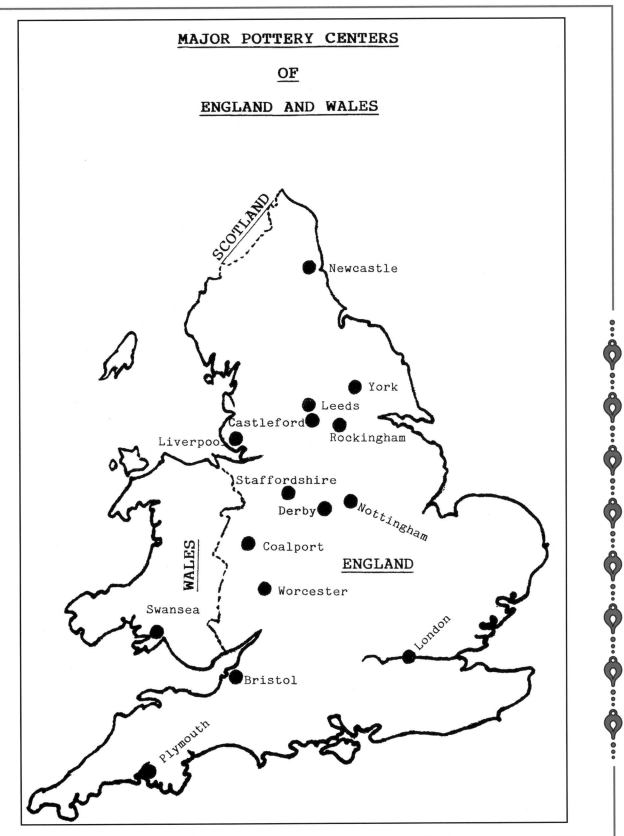

The opening of the Mersey and Trent canal in 1777 was a boon for Staffordshire potters. With shipping costs of raw materials now a fraction of what they had been, English potters could now compete with Chinese porcelains.

Tureens are usually found in two sizes: sauce and soup. Sauce tureens are small, averaging 6 to 7 inches in length, while soup tureens are double that in length. The general shape of both is either oval or rectangular. All tureens came with lids that had a piece cut out for the ladle handle. Ladles and undertrays for tureens were sold separately. The ubiquitous platter was often employed as an undertray for soup tureens. Bodies are pearlware or creamware. Edge colors are usually blue or green. C. 1775 – 1830.

Rare Wedgwood Mared round tureen with separate undertray. 8" high x 8¼" d. **$1,000.00 and up.**

Sauce tureen with attached under-tray and rococo style handles. **$450.00 – 550.00.**

Eighteenth century soup tureen, with family monogram in underglaze black.
$1,000.00 and up.

Sauce tureen, having no need of handles because of small size and
attached undertray. Great green shell edge decoration. **$450.00 –
550.00**.

Soup tureens, each, **$850.00 and up**.

Sauce tureen with oversized, flaring handles and attached undertray. Rare two-tone blue decoration on ends of undertray. With lid, **$500.00 – 600.00**.

Soup tureen, without platter, **$850.00 and up**.

Soup tureen, without platter, **$850.00 and up**.

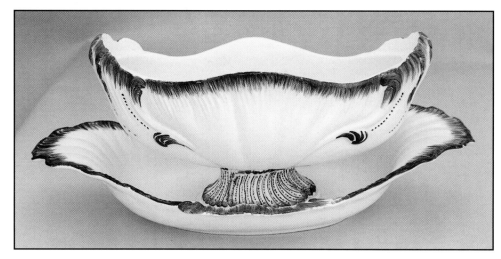

Rare example of rococo cobalt decoration on faience (tin-glazed earthenware) soup tureen. Marked "ESTE," Padua, Italy, c.1750 – 1850. Attached undertray. The company may have been trying to copy Wedgwood since he produced a very similar style with similar decoration c.1775. Length of tureen, 11¾", height, 6½". With lid, **$850.00 and up.**

Sauce tureens, each, **$375.00 – 500.00.**

Wedgwood Mared soup tureen, without platter, **$1,000.00 and up.**

The workmanship on this tureen is exquisite. Large, foliated handle terminals are picked out in blue and the edge is of shell quality. Even the handles have a delicate cobalt design of a vine with leaves. No opening in the lid for a ladle denotes that this tureen was for service of dry ingredients. The size is between that of a sauce tureen and a soup tureen. 9¾" long. **$750.00 – 900.00.**

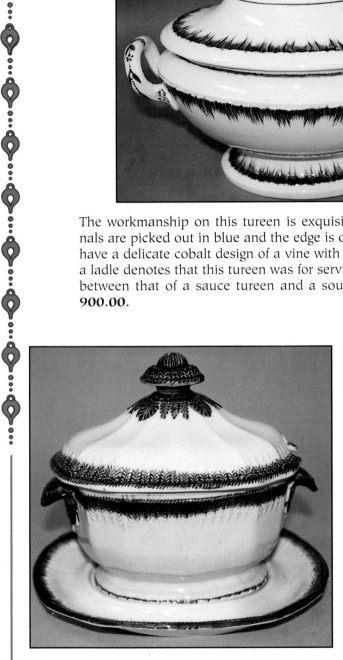

Although a gravy tureen, this Rogers piece is larger than the average size. The panelled sides are unusual. Separate undertray. Without undertray, **$550.00 – 650.00**.

Another oddly sized soup tureen, 10 inches long. Squatty form with ornate, solid cobalt handles and life-size flower finial. Molded peg-like feet. Although marked "WOOD" and attributable to Enoch Wood, there were several potters who used this mark. **$850.00 – 950.00**.

A master salt is a small bowl, generally set on a pedestal base. They are usually 3" to 3½" in diameter and 2" to 3" high. The bowl is rounded or straight-sided (although these are much less common). Double salts, or salt cellars, were also made. The bodies are pearlware and are found with blue or green rim color. C. 1780 – 1830.

Pepper pots, or castors, are 4" to 5½" high and were manufactured in a wide variety of shapes. There is almost always a rim beneath the holes. Pepper has been the most popular spice for thousands of years. It was so much in demand during the Middle Ages that it had the nickname "black gold." Pepper pots were often part of a castor stand containing two or three pepper pots, two or three bottles and possibly a mustard. The stand could be decorated as well. Bodies were pearlware and, rarely, creamware, usually with blue or green edges. Decorative painting (in the same color as the edge) on the top of the pot is not uncommon. Some pepper pots will have a ball-shaped finial. C. 1790 – 1820.

Mustard, along with pepper and salt, was one of the three most used spices of the period. Mustard, being the cheapest, was the most frequently served. By the eighteenth century it was served as a paste rather than dry. Spoons used were wooden; wet mustard had corrosive qualities, due to the vinegar, so metal spoons were not used. There is no evidence of the existence of ceramic spoons. Mustard pots were made in a variety of shapes and sizes. Most are a few inches high and a few inches wide. All had lids with an opening for a spoon. Rarely, they are found with stands (undertrays). The bodies are pearlware, bordering on whiteware at times. They are found with blue or green edges. C.1800 – 1830.

Master Salts

A rare example of a rococo style master salt with curved "legs" and paw feet. It is easy to date this piece by studying furniture styles of the period. Also rare is the overhanging lip. **$550.00 – 650.00.**

Each, **$350.00 – 450.00**.

A group of master salts, featuring a rare footless master salt with an angular body, second from left. Each, **$350.00 – 450.00**.

Three rare master salts in the rococo style, fluted, elliptical bowls with diamond-shaped pedestals. Two have polychrome decoration. Plain, **$450.00 – 550.00**. Decorated, each, **$550.00 – 650.00**.

Rare master salt with cover. Leeds Pottery produced these in plain creamware. **$475.00 – 550.00.**

Pepper Pots

Each, **$175.00 – 275.00.**

Rare creamware pepper pot with overglaze painting in aqua, and pearlware pot with molded green edges and pointed cap, each, **$295.00 – 395.00.**

The straight-sided form, ball finial, and heavy cobalt decoration set this pot apart from others. The impressed "R" on the base is impossible to attribute to one potter. **$295.00 – 395.00.**

Mustard Pots

Although a pepper pot form, the top was made to be detachable, and a piece cut out for a spoon. Rare. **$400.00 – 500.00.**

The most typical form for the feather edge mustard pot, **$250.00 – 350.00.**

The pear-shaped form shown here is harder to find. The cobalt edge is molded on the pot at left, and underglaze blue on the remaining two. Each, with lids, **$275.00 – 350.00.**

Pear-shaped mustard pot with lid, decorative handle treatment. Shown with wooden and porcelain spoons. **$275.00 – 350.00.**

Ladles

Ladles were made in two sizes, to fit either sauce tureens or soup tureens. The sauce tureen length is about 7" and the soup tureen length can vary from 10" to 14". Ladles usually have pearlware bodies. Most have a blue edge. The outer rim of the bowl is decorated and sometimes the stem is, too. They were easily broken and are very hard to find. C.1775 – 1830.

Back, soup ladle, **$550.00 – 650.00**. Front, sauce ladle, **$300.00 – 400.00**.

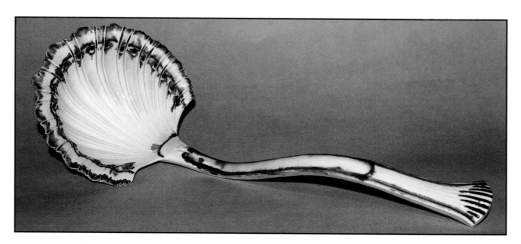

Rococo ladle with Mared pattern (although possibly not made by Wedgwood, due to the lack of quality in the Mared pattern). Note the shell influence. Rare. **$850.00 and up.**

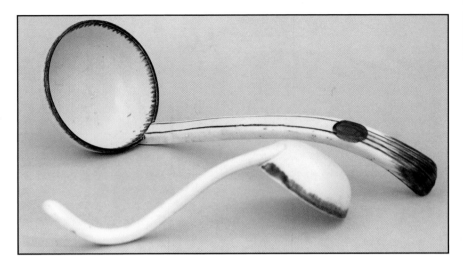

Back, soup, **$550.00 –
650.00**. Front, sauce,
$300.00 – 400.00.

Soup ladle with
undecorated shell
bowl and fluted stem;
ladles with similar
bowls were made by
Turner. **$850.00 and
up**.

The stem of this soup
ladle mirrors similarly
decorated plates and
platters of the same
time period. This is a
rare treatment for a
feather edge ladle.
$595.00 – 695.00.

Cups and Mugs

    Cups and mugs are rare forms in feather edge. Cups were often handleless; with one handle or two, they could be quite fancy, with twined straps and foliated (leaf) terminals, due to their date of production. Matching saucers are not evident. This is partly due to the low number of cups and saucers originally manufactured, as tea cups and saucers were part of a tea service. Also, pieces thought of as small plates today may have been used as saucers originally; there was no indentation for a cup. The mugs shown here are very small, which may be referred to as child size. Some mugs (also referred to as coffee cans) had saucers. Tea and coffee were drunk by all, but the fashionable also drank chocolate in the eighteenth century. Cups and mugs are found in creamware and pearlware, and with blue or, rarely, green edges. C. 1790 – 1820.

Mug with embossed cobalt edge. The embossed edge on this mug, a fine vertical rib, is also found on mustard pots, master salts, and coffee pots. It was produced by using a tool similar to a pastry crimper. **$350.00 – 450.00**

Pearlware cups shown with whiteware cup plates. Cups, each, **$250.00 – 300.00.**

Cup, without small plate, **$250.00 – 275.00**. Custard or chocolate cup, "clouded" band at rim. Probably Leeds Pottery, about 1770. **$275.00 – 350.00**.

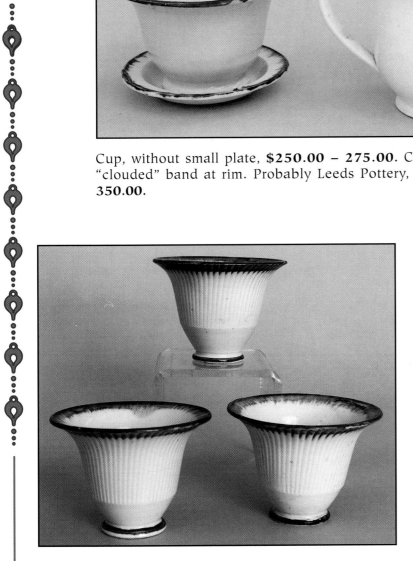

Fluted cups (possibly, the fluted sides were to facilitate holding the cup), **$250.00 – 300.00 each**.

More shallow than the mug on page 30, this green-edge mug measures 1⅝" high x 2⅝" in diameter. **$350.00 – 450.00**.

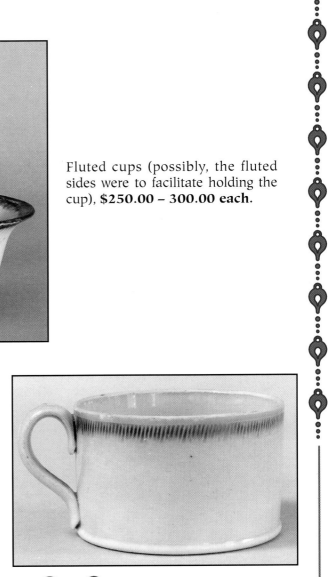

Plates are second to platters in being the most common form. They are the one form made from the beginning to the very end of feather edge production; a collection of them could showcase every possible edge, color, and type of decoration. They were a canvas for the potter's art.

The size of a plate determines its use. Cup plates, to place under cups to protect a table surface, are under 4½" in diameter. These are found in pearlware and whiteware. Salad and toddy plates are from 4½" to under 7½" in diameter. These are found in all three body types. Luncheon and dinner plates measure 7½" and up. The largest size for any plate is about 10½". The larger plates are also found in all three body types. Soup plates measure from 8" to 10" in diameter and are usually found only in pearlware and whiteware. C. 1770 – 1900.

Whiteware, embossed and painted edge. Toddy size, **$65.00 – 85.00**, large, **$35.00 – 55.00**.

Plates, 8", green (copper oxide) rim, marked "CHOISY LE ROY" and "CHAN-TILLY," both French, c.1800. **$100.00 – 135.00 each**.

This edge is referred to as Fishscale and Feather. Toddy size, **$95.00 – 125.00**.

Dinner plate with evenly scalloped shell edge. **$165.00 – 225.00**.

Rare whiteware toddy-size plate with red embossed edge, **$175.00 – 250.00**.

Embossed-edge dinner plates. This is the typical pearlware dinner plate you will find at antique shows. These plates can also be found in smaller sizes; prices will descend with size. Dinner plates, each, **$150.00 – 250.00**.

Dinner plate with rare mulberry transfer of Charity (transfers tend to be in the same color as the edge), **$350.00 – 450.00**.

Rare brown-edge dinner plate with ship and floral transfers, **$450.00 – 550.00**.

Presentation cup plate, "A Present from a Friend." Many transferware pieces, feather edge or not, have genre scenes. **$375.00 – 450.00**.

Polychrome-decorated dinner plate, Pratt colors. **$375.00 – 550.00**.

Embossed-edge soup plate. **$150.00 – 250.00**, depending on size.

Rare shell edge dinner plate with underglaze blue Chinoiserie design. All four design elements are present, the house, fence, birds, and Long Eliza. Diameter, 9¾". **$395.00 – 500.00.**

Polychrome decorated dinner-size plate. This design can also be found on feather edge platters and chargers. **$550.00 – 750.00.**

Rare dessert plate decorated for Wedgwood by Guy Green (the Green of Sadler and Green) of Liverpool. Printed in dark brown with a bright green enamel wash. The rim is an example of an asymmetrical edge with a plain band. Josiah Wedgwood was not happy with the strong coloring, although he conceded that the coloring would be acceptable to the "foreigners" for whom it was intended. C.1777 – 1978. Each, **$550.00 – 650.00.**

Rare red shell edge plate with an exceptionally delicate hand-painted, polychrome design of atypical colors. **$450.00 – 550.00.**

Polychrome decorated 7" plate, **$375.00 – 450.00**.

Wedgwood Mared shell edge dinner plates. Wedgwood still uses this size for the dinner plates it produces currently. Each, **$250.00 – 350.00**.

"Pine Tree" border dinner plate. Embossed edge with further rim molding. This design is hard to find and is usually found in cobalt. Flat pieces, such as plates and platters, seem to be the extent of production for this molded design. Blue, **$225.00 – 275.00**. Green, **$250.00 – 295.00**.

Irregular or asymmetrical edge in rare mulberry coloring. Creamware; dinner plate size. **$200.00 – 275.00**.

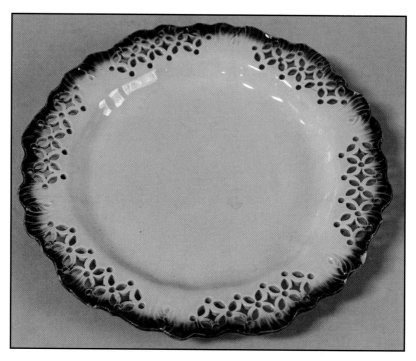

Seven-inch asymmetrical blue-edge plate with reticulated (netlike) rim. C. 1780. **$275.00 – 350.00**.

Octagonal toddy plate, polychrome "berries." Octagonal plates of any size, with or without decoration, are very hard to find. **$450.00 – 550.00**

Rare brown shell-edge plate with brown Chinoiserie design and pumpkin slip band. Attributed to the Don Pottery. **$400.00 and up.**

Green edge soup plate with embossed swag rim. Further rim embossing shows a rarely seen design of cornucopias and shells. **$250.00 – 300.00**.

This 9½" pearlware plate is exceptional in many ways. The rare red feathering is heavy on an unusual geometric edge. The crisp green scenic transfer, generically referred to as Romantic Staffordshire, is unique at this time in conjunction with feather edge. **$450.00 – 550.00**.

Platters

Platters are the commonest form in feather edge. Most platters are found in larger sizes, making the smaller ones unusual. The larger platters make sense, of course, as the English ate huge quantities of meat, as much as a 30-pound joint at dinner in a large household. No vessel was ever used on the table without some type of platter or undertray, another reason for the high number of platters found. Creamware platters, however, are not common, as most feather edge platters are pearlware or ironstone. The shape of a platter can determine the age and clay body. Creamware platters are oval or elliptical in shape, while ironstone platters are usually rectangular with cut, or chamfered, corners. Pearlware platters are found in every shape. C. 1770 – c. 1900.

Green embossed and shell edge pearlware platters. Each, **$250.00 – 350.00**.

Blue shell edge pearlware platters. Each, **$150.00 – 275.00**.

Rare ironstone red edge platter, feathered and slightly embossed edge, **$450.00 – 500.00**.

Rare well and tree platter, blue edge, **$400.00 – 500.00**.

Bottom of platter above.

Wedgwood Mared shell edge platters. Note the elliptical shape, in keeping with their age. Each, **$450.00 – 550.00**.

Creamware rococo platters or undertrays, 13¼" long. Rare black overglaze feathering with narrow aqua outer edge. Each, **$550.00 – 650.00**.

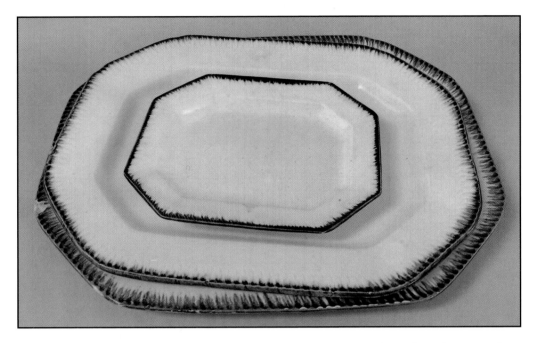

These three blue edge platters are the standard ironstone form found. Depending on size, prices can range from **$75.00 – 250.00**.

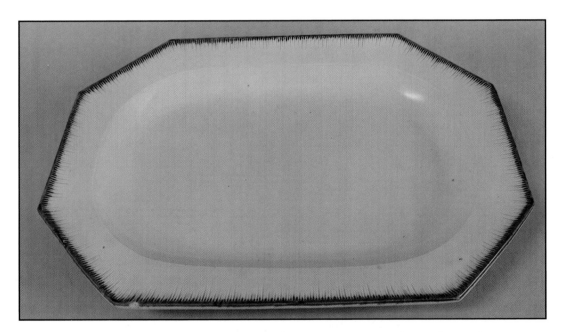

Octagonal forms in pearlware are rare, platters even more than plates. **$300.00 – 400.00**.

This section encompasses a wide variety of shapes and sizes. These vessels were used to serve anything from sauces to meats to pickled cauliflower. All body types and edge colors are found. C.1775 – 1880.

Diamond-shaped, pearlware dishes such as this one can be found in a range of sizes. **$275.00 up**, depending on size.

Round serving dishes are less common than their rectangular counterparts. Left, about 7", whiteware, **$125.00 – 175.00**. Right, 12", pearlware with embossed edge, **$250.00 – 300.00**.

Rare creamware elliptical dessert dish with black rococo edge and black enamel transfer of Minerva, goddess of wisdom and the arts. Probably decorated by Sadler and Green of Liverpool, who were known for black transfer printing on creamware. **$450.00 – 600.00**.

Wedgwood, shallow (under 2") serving dishes with Mared pattern. One of the uses of these dishes was serving fruit. Each one is 9½ to 11½" long. Each, **$550.00 – 650.00**.

Rare creamware elliptical compote with separate undertray, red shell edge. Compote is 1¾" tall, tray is 5½" long. **$650.00 and up**.

Wedgwood charger, Mared pattern. 17½" diameter, 1½" deep. **$650.00 and up**.

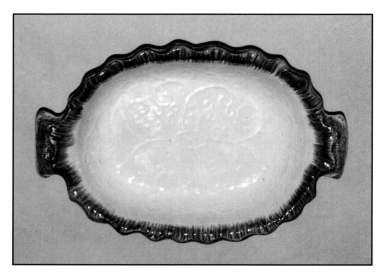

Oblong pearlware dish with handles, serving area finely embossed in a scroll design, 5" long. **$225.00 – 325.00**

This square dish with cover was referred to by Wedgwood as a "root dish;" others called it a "ragoo" (sic) dish. Ragout is a highly seasoned stew with meat and vegetables. The manufacture of a dish for ragout shows the heavy influence of the French on English cuisine at this time. 10½" square, 5¼" high. **$650.00 – 850.00.**

Oval and elliptical Mared serving dishes. The Mared pattern has an unexplained origin. The design most closely resembles a Meissen "onion" pattern. Each, **$450.00 – 600.00**.

This small, shell-shaped pearlware dish would have been used for desserts. **$300.00 – 400.00**.

Rare pearlware square, open dish, probably used for salad. **$350.00 – 450.00.**

Beautiful creamware bowl, probably part of a dessert set. Asymmetrical mulberry edge. Marked Wedgwood (mid-1760s), possibly decorated by Bakewell, who was known for using the mulberry, or purple, color on his work. 10 " x 7½" x 1" high. Shown with plates. Bowl, **$450.00 – 550.00.**

Scalloped and embossed oval fruit bowl. These dishes, called compotiers by Wedgwood, were made in round and oval shapes; each shape was made in six sizes, from 7" to 12". **$300.00 – 400.00.**

Large round bowls. Left, blue edge whiteware with beaded edge, **$250.00 – 350.00.** Right, green edge pearlware with embossed edge, **$300.00 – 400.00.**

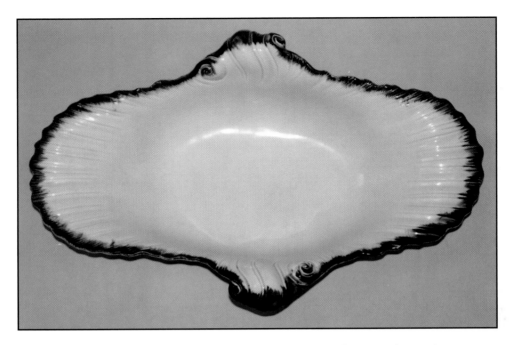

Rare dessert dish, scrolled handles. Deep cobalt edge, 11" long. **$350.00 – 450.00**.

Heavy, ironstone oval bowls. These were made near the end of feather edge production, as there is no molding whatsoever. **$100.00 – 275.00**, depending on size.

Rare small dish, divided into quarters. Considering that it is under 2" in depth, it was probably used for various kinds of pickles. Blue, asymmetrical edge. Marked "TURNER". C.1790. **$550.00 – 650.00.**

Round, covered ragout dish in blue edge pearlware. Ragout dishes were shown in many shapes, at least 10, and up to 5 sizes, in the 1817 Wedgwood catalog. Realistic dogwood blossom finial. 11½" long x 6½" high. **$600.00 – 795.00.**

This octagonal shape is the most common form for ironstone serving dishes. Depending on size, **$100.00 – 275.00**.

Leaf dishes: These small, leaf-shaped dishes shown in next six photos were used for desserts and pickled vegetables. A few have peg feet or flat bottoms, indicating c. 1800, but they are usually found with a molded foot rim. The average length is 6". Most are pearlware with a blue edge. They would make an interesting collection. **$175.00 – 325.00 each**, depending on size, edge color, age, and surface decoration.

Many leaf dishes have a realistic molded design on their interior surface; sometimes the molded design is picked out in blue. Marked examples are rare. Each, **$175.00 –350.00**.

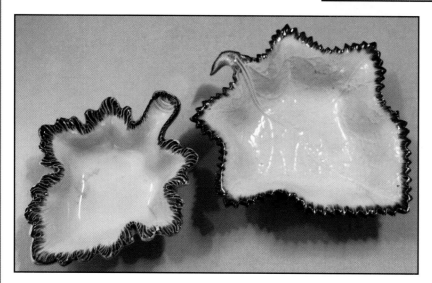

Pairs of leaf dishes are rarely found. Both of these pairs have peg feet, indicating their date of manufacture as c. 1800. Pair, **$550.00 – 700.00**.

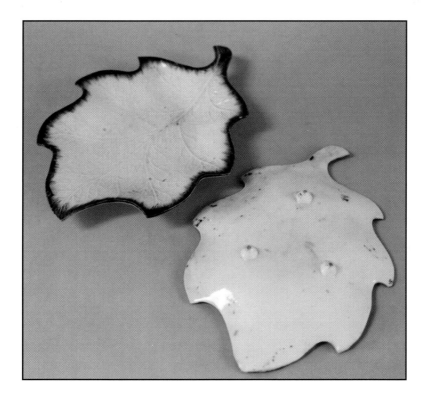

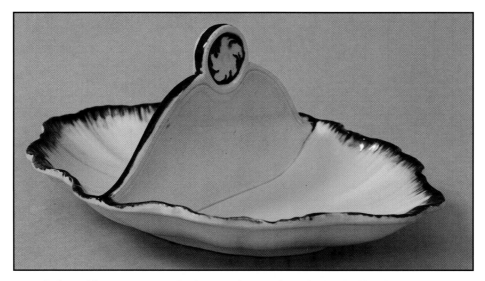

Divided pickle server, made by Wedgwood. Cobalt shell edge with cobalt detailing on the divider and molded, disc-shaped handle. Pickle servers were produced with two, three, or four sections. 6" long. **$500.00 – 600.00**.

Round covered vegetable dish, 7" diameter. The body is pearlware bordering on whiteware. Applied open handles. **$600.00 and up**.

Pierced, or reticulated, drainers were meant to be inserted into a platter to drain off meat juices. They are an earlier form and are found mostly in pearlware; a few creamware ones exist as well. Their shapes tend be rectangular with rounded corners, following the shape of most platters; in these as well, shape determines age. Generally blue edge. C.1775 – 1820.

Rare round drainer, Wedgwood Mared pattern. Diameter 12⅝". Shown with the large Mared charger also on page 52. Notice the highly decorative piercing: shaped holes, as well as placement of the holes. **$750.00 and up**.

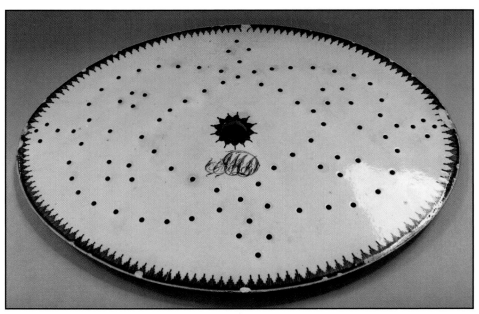

Creamware elliptical drainer with overglaze brick-red monogram. Note the interesting edge, a finely painted sawtooth pattern. Marked "HERCULA-NEUM," c.1800. **$350.00 – 450.00**.

Many foods were served sauced, hence the need for so many sauceboats. The earliest sauce-boats were a mirror image of silver forms in use at the time. Sauceboats sometimes had under-trays, attached or not. Pearlware bodies predominate; most sauceboats are found with a blue edge of some type. C.1775 – 1830.

The average feather edge sauceboat is 6" to 7" in length. Blue edge, each, **$100.00 – 200.00**, depending on size and amount of decoration. Note the flat foot on the sauceboat on the left, as opposed to the applied and decorated foot on the sauceboat on the right. Green silver-form sauce-boat with stand, **$275.00 – 350.00**.

Wedgwood Mared sauceboats in a silver form. Average length 8½". Sauceboat, each, **$300.00 – 400.00**. Undertray, 6" x 8⅝". **$200.00 – 250.00**.

Vase, blue asymmetrical rim with underglaze blue transfer, showing a neoclassical scene, liberty cap, and floral sheet transfers. 6¾" high. C.1790 – 1820. **$550.00 and up**, depending on size.

Back of vase on preceding page.

Blue-edge pearlware food mold of a flower. Also found with a green edge. 6" x 5¼". C. 1820 – 1830. **$500.00 and up**.

Wedgwood Mared strawberry basket and stand. Note the scalloped interior of the stand, to follow the scalloped exterior of the basket. The basket measures 4¼" x 5⅞" x 5⅛" high. The stand measures 7⅞" x 6¾". **$1,450.00 and up**.

Toy dishes; Pieces like these are so small that they are easily overlooked. The plates are barely bigger than a half-dollar. Toy dishes are early, with shell edges or overglaze feathering, usually in blue. These pieces are part of a dinner service. Hollow pieces such as tureens and ragout dishes can also be found. C. 1810 – 1830. 2¼" diameter, and platter, 4¼" long, each, **$100.00 – 150.00.** Sauceboat, 2¾" long, with separate undertray, **$250.00 –350.00.** (Shown with a full-size sauceboat for scale.)

Incredible! One of the earliest toy services known, this creamware tea service is shown on the cover of Doris Anderson Lechler's *English Toy China*. The cobalt feathering is overglaze and very finely done. In addition to the usual pieces found in a tea service, this set has a tea caddy with a cover and a cakestand. The coffeepot is the largest piece at 5" high. Other pieces are tea caddy, 3½" high; cakestand, 1¼" high; and cream pitcher, 3½" high. C. 1770 – 1780. **$7,500.00 and up.**

Ironstone cakestand with feathered cobalt edge and floral transfers. Staffordshire, England, c. 1900. Height, 4¼ ", width 8¾". **$150.00 – 200.00.**

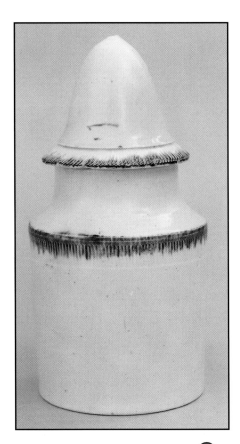

Pearlware condiment container with cover, from a cruet stand. Height, 5". Also found in green-edge. C.1790 – 1810. **$300.00 – 375.00.**

These two pieces illustrate the use of feather edge as an auxiliary decoration.

Any plant would be honored to be housed in this polychromed/blue edge flower pot. 4¼" high. C.1810 – 1830. **$950.00 and up.**

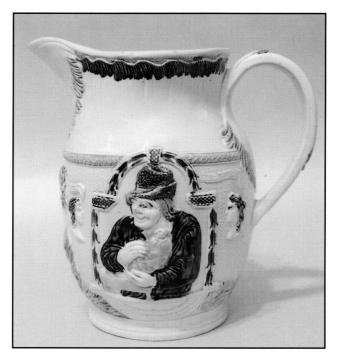

Pearlware jug with embossed and polychromed "Shakespeare" design; great blue shell edge decorating the rim, spout, and handle. C.1800 – 1820. **$1,000.00 and up.**

Top and bottom of pearlware platter with hot-water base and reticulated surface. Plates can be found with the hot-water section on the bottom, but one wonders whether the purpose of this piece was to keep food hot or drain off juices. Incredible reticulation! C.1790 – 1810. **$750.00 and up.**

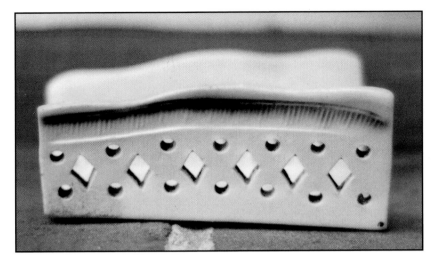

Pearlware reticulated asparagus server with embossed green edge.
$350.00 – 450.00.

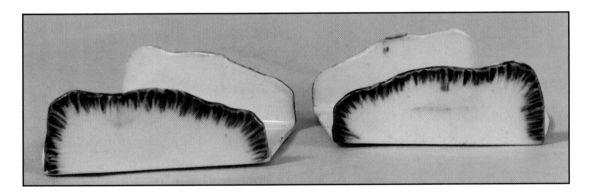

Drawings from one of Josiah Wedgwood's shape books show four asparagus servers on an oval platter, placed at right angles. The servers were meant to hold four or more stalks, for individual servings. The bottoms are about 3" x 3" and sides are 1" high. The servers are narrower at the front. Rarely found. C. 1719 – c. 1810. **$350.00 – 450.00 each**.

Shell edges are obviously not confined to plain white earthenware. The pitcher above in yellow-glazed white earthenware has a black shell edge and black freehand decoration; the yellow-glazed quintal vase below has an uncolored shell edge. C.1790 – 1810. Each, **$1,000.00 and up**

Pearlware egg cups are also found in green-edge. Some egg cups had lids and were sold in sets. C.1800 – 1830. **$295.00 – 395.00**.

This Mared bottle would have been part of a cruet stand or an oil and vinegar stand. A miniscule pottery stopper with a ball finial would have served as a lid. 4¼" high. **$350.00 – 425.00**.

Wedgwood rococo cobalt-edge pearlware coffee pot. This piece still retains some of its original oil gilt highlights. Gilding was usually done to highlight an already colored edge; rarely, it is the sole edge color. 9½" tall. C.1775 – 1790. **$1,500.00 and up.**

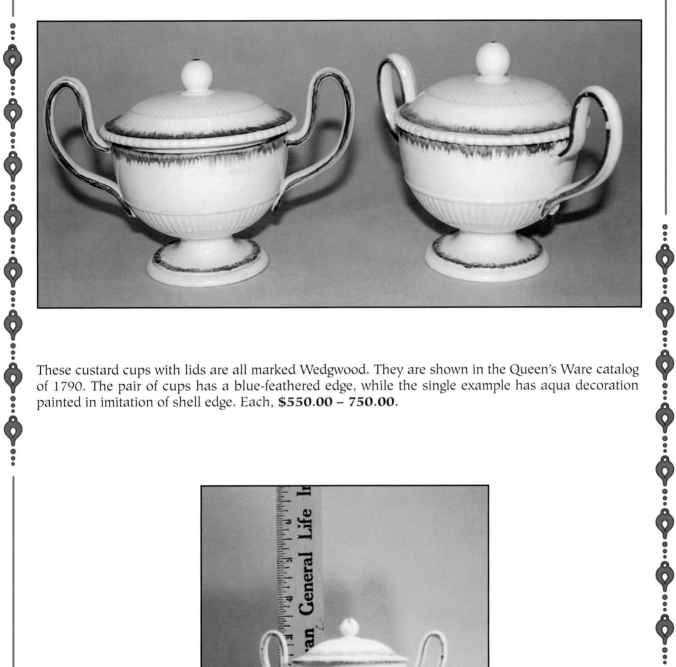

These custard cups with lids are all marked Wedgwood. They are shown in the Queen's Ware catalog of 1790. The pair of cups has a blue-feathered edge, while the single example has aqua decoration painted in imitation of shell edge. Each, **$550.00 – 750.00.**

Covered milk pitcher in the Mared pattern, part of a tea service. It retains some of its original gilding. 6½" tall. **$950.00 and up.**

This ewer, from a pitcher and bowl set, has a molded and feathered rim combined with straight blue bands. 7¾" high. C.1820 – 1830. **$650.00 – 800.00**.

Creamware soup tureen lid, rococo draped edge with underglaze blue freehand decoration. Rope twist foliated handle. C.1780. Lid only, **$200.00 – 250.00**.

Pair of quintal vases. Found in pairs or singles, these five-fingered, pearlware vases were useful for displaying tulips (all the rage about 1800). The underglaze blue decoration is typical of the period. Quintal vases can also be found plain or with polychrome decoration. 8" tall with a 9" spread. Pair, **$1,250.00 and up.**

Pearlware teapot stand, cobalt edge, draped "skirt," paw feet. C.1780. **$750.00 and up**.

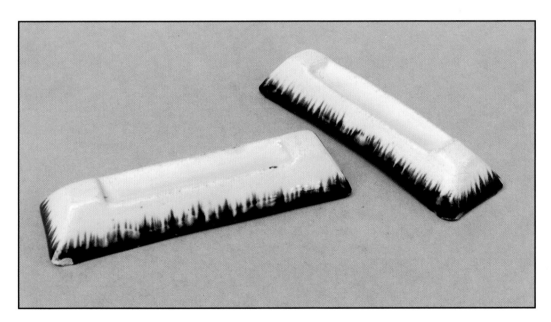

Pearlware knife rests with a cobalt feather edge, 4" long. C.1800. Each, **$350.00 – 450.00**.

Feather edge baskets resemble a woven splint basket. Some are cut and molded from a single sheet of clay with various reticulations. Others are woven from strips of clay; these were also called twig baskets. All had matching undertrays or stands. Baskets were produced mainly for fruit, sometimes for sweetmeats. Sweetmeats were the candy of the day, not our typical chocolate, but candied flowers, marzipan, etc. C.1780 – c. 1820. With or without stand, **$750.00 and up each.**

"Canoe" fruit basket, pearlware with blue edge. Shown in Wedgwood's 1817 catalog. 11" x 6½" x 4" high.

Elliptical basket and stand, marked SPODE.

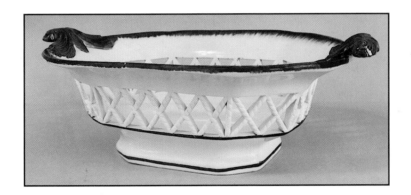

Undertray (stand). These can be found alone and are decorative in their own right. This stand is marked Neale & Co. **$150.00 – 250.00**.

This is a hot plate. The reservoir under the plate's surface was filled with hot water and kept the food on the plate warm. Asymmetrical blue edge on pearlware, 9¾" diameter, 2" deep. C. 1790. **$475.00 – 600.00**.

Artichoke custard cups with lids, pearlware with green edge. 3½" high. These were made by Wedgwood. C. 1785 – 1790. Each, **$450.00 – 550.00**.

These small, eighteenth-century dishes with a blue shell edge were intended for serving pickled vegetables. The crescent-shaped dish may have been one of four small dishes, forming an ellipse around a central dish, and produced by Wedgwood. The bell-shaped dish is 4½" long. Each, **$300.00 – 400.00**.

Reproductions of feather edge can be found, produced mostly by Wedgwood. It is a good idea to own a few reproductions as part of the education process. Marks can be sanded off the bottom of a piece, and if you are not familiar with what you are buying, you can be fooled. It is also vital to own books showing pottery marks, since ceramics can be dated by marks. All pieces shown are marked.

Shell edge plate with handpainted polychrome flowers, made by Wedgwood in 1929.

This shell edge china was made in the 1950s and 1960s by Wedgwood, exclusively for Colonial Williamsburg. The edges were dark blue or dark green. Dinner and tea services were both produced. The pieces shown are a small sampling of the available forms.

Cup and saucer from the previous group, showing both edge colors.

These candlesticks are copies, originally made by Wedgwood, c.1785. They were made in Italy for Mottahedah and sold in the Winterthur gift shop. C.1970s.

Bibliography

Burton, William, *Josiah Wedgwood and His Pottery* (Cassell and Company, Ltd., London, 1922).

Dunne, Patrick J., *Everything Nice* (Southern Accents, Southern Progress Corp., Birmingham, AL, Sept.-Oct. 1999, pp. 90 – 98).

Fenelly, Catherine, *Staffordshire on American Tables: The Collamore Evidence* (Antiques, Straight Enterprises, Inc., NYC, July 1963, pp. 75 – 79).

Godden, Geoffrey A., *An Illustrated Encyclopedia of British Pottery and Porcelain* (Bonanza Books, NYC, n.d.).

Hunter, Robert R. Jr. and George L. Miller, *English Shell-Edge Earthenware* (The Magazine Antiques, Brant Publications, Inc.,NYC, March 1994, pp. 433 – 443).

Lechler, Doris Anderson, *English Toy China* (Antique Publications, Marietta, Ohio, 1989).

Lewis, John and Griselda, *Pratt Ware English and Scottish Relief Decorated and Underglaze Coloured Earthenware 1780 – 1840* (Baron Publishing, Woodbridge, Suffolk,1984).

Noel-Hume, Ivor, *A Guide to Artifacts of Colonial America* (Alfred K. Knopf, NYC, 1969, pp.102 – 138).

Noel-Hume, Ivor, *Pearlware: Forgotten Milestone of English Ceramic History* (Antiques, Straight Enterprises, Inc; NYC, March 1969, pp. 390 – 397).

Noel-Hume, Ivor, *The Rise and Fall of English White Salt-Glazed Stoneware Part I* (Antiques, Straight Enterprises, Inc., NYC, February 1970, pp. 248 – 255).

Noel-Hume, Ivor, *The Rise and Fall of English White Salt-Glazed Stoneware Part II* (Antiques, Straight Enterprises, Inc., NYC, March 1970, pp. 408 – 413).

Noel-Hume, Ivor, *The What, Who, and When of English Plate Design* (The Magazine Antiques, Straight Enterprises, Inc., February 1973, pp. 350-355).

Quimby, Ian M. G. (Ed.) *Ceramics in America* (Winterthur Museum, Inc., The University Press of Virginia, Charlottesville, 1973).

Reilly, Robin and George Savage, *The Dictionary Of Wedgwood* (Antique Collectors' Club Ltd., Suffolk, England, 1985, Reprinted 1989).

Walton, Peter, *Creamware and Other English Pottery at Temple Newsam House Leeds* (Manningham Press, London, 1976).

Weatherbee, Jean, *A Second Look at White Ironstone* (Wallace-Homestead, Lombard, IL, 1985).

Williams, Petra, *Staffordshire Romantic Transfer Patterns* (Fountain House East, Jeffersontown, KY, 1978).

COLLECTOR'S
GUIDE TO

Yellow Ware

An Identification & Value Guide

Lisa S.
McAllister

ISBN: 0-89145-741-0 • #4734 • 8.5 x 11
128 Pgs. PB • $17.95

Yellow ware was produced for over a century and played an important part in pottery history. Its popularity on the collector's market has brought about much new information in recent years. Lisa McAllister reveals the latest knowledge and introduces pieces that have never been in print before in her Collector's Guide to Yellow Ware. There are over 300 full-color photographs, with descriptions, sizes, and current values. There's an unbelievable variety of yellow ware illustrated in this book — the collector will find anything from an 1830s miniature flower pot to a 1930s banded pitcher. The pieces are categorized by type, demonstrating that yellow ware wasn't just utilitarian kitchen ware. Besides the bowls, plates, pitchers, and storage crocks, there are inkwells, banks, animal figures, and much more! There's also an informative section on the potters and their marks, a glossary, and a bibliography. This exceptional guide will be a bonus for all pottery libraries. For only $17.95, it's a great buy!

COLLECTOR BOOKS
A Division of Schroeder Publishing Co., Inc.

COLLECTOR BOOKS

Informing Today's Collector

For over two decades we have been keeping collectors informed on trends and values in all fields of antiques and collectibles.

DOLLS, FIGURES & TEDDY BEARS

4707	A Decade of **Barbie Dolls** & Collectibles, 1981–1991, Summers	$19.95
4631	**Barbie Doll** Boom, 1986–1995, Augustyniak	$18.95
2079	**Barbie Doll** Fashion, Volume I, Eames	$24.95
4846	**Barbie Doll** Fashion, Volume II, Eames	$24.95
3957	**Barbie** Exclusives, Rana	$18.95
4632	**Barbie** Exclusives, Book II, Rana	$18.95
4557	**Barbie,** The First 30 Years, Deutsch	$24.95
5672	The **Barbie Doll** Years, 4th Ed., Olds	$19.95
3810	**Chatty Cathy** Dolls, Lewis	$15.95
5352	Collector's Ency. of **Barbie** Doll Exclusives & More, 2nd Ed.,Augustyniak	$24.95
2211	Collector's Encyclopedia of **Madame Alexander** Dolls, Smith	$24.95
4863	Collector's Encyclopedia of **Vogue Dolls**, Izen/Stover	$29.95
5598	**Doll Values**, Antique to Modern, 4th Ed., Moyer	$12.95
56101	**Madame Alexander** Collector's Dolls Price Guide #25, Crowsey	$9.95
5612	**Modern Collectible Dolls**, Volume IV, Moyer	$24.95
5365	**Peanuts Collectibles**, Podley/Bang	$24.95
5253	Story of **Barbie**, 2nd Ed., Westenhouser	$24.95
5277	**Talking Toys** of the 20th Century, Lewis	$15.95
1513	**Teddy Bears & Steiff** Animals, Mandel	$9.95
1817	**Teddy Bears & Steiff** Animals, 2nd Series, Mandel	$19.95
2084	**Teddy Bears, Annalee's & Steiff** Animals, 3rd Series, Mandel	$19.95
5371	**Teddy Bear** Treasury, Yenke	$19.95
1808	Wonder of **Barbie**, Manos	$9.95
1430	World of **Barbie** Dolls, Manos	$9.95
4880	World of **Raggedy Ann** Collectibles, Avery	$24.95

TOYS, MARBLES & CHRISTMAS COLLECTIBLES

2333	Antique & Collectible **Marbles**, 3rd Ed., Grist	$9.95
5353	**Breyer Animal** Collector's Guide, 2nd Ed., Browell	$19.95
4976	**Christmas Ornaments**, Lights & Decorations, Johnson	$24.95
4737	**Christmas Ornaments**, Lights & Decorations, Vol. II, Johnson	$24.95
4739	**Christmas Ornaments**, Lights & Decorations, Vol. III, Johnson	$24.95
4649	Classic Plastic **Model Kits**, Polizzi	$24.95
4559	Collectible **Action Figures**, 2nd Ed., Manos	$17.95
3874	Collectible **Coca-Cola Toy Trucks**, deCourtivron	$24.95
2338	Collector's Encyclopedia of **Disneyana**, Longest, Stern	$24.95
4958	Collector's Guide to **Battery Toys**, Hultzman	$19.95
5038	Collector's Guide to **Diecast Toys** & Scale Models, 2nd Ed., Johnson	$19.95
4651	Collector's Guide to **Tinker Toys**, Strange	$18.95
4566	Collector's Guide to **Tootsietoys**, 2nd Ed., Richter	$19.95
5169	Collector's Guide to **TV Toys** & Memorabilia, 2nd Ed., Davis/Morgan	$24.95
5360	**Fisher-Price Toys**, Cassity	$19.95
4720	The Golden Age of **Automotive Toys**, 1925–1941, Hutchison/Johnson	$24.95
5593	Grist's Big Book of **Marbles**, 2nd Ed.	$24.95
3970	Grist's Machine-Made & Contemporary **Marbles**, 2nd Ed.	$9.95
5267	**Matchbox Toys**, 1947 to 1998, 3rd Ed., Johnson	$19.95
4871	**McDonald's** Collectibles, Henriques/DuVall	$19.95
1540	Modern **Toys** 1930–1980, Baker	$19.95
3888	**Motorcycle Toys**, Antique & Contemporary, Gentry/Downs	$18.95
5368	**Schroeder's Collectible Toys**, Antique to Modern Price Guide, 6th Ed.	$17.95
2028	**Toys**, Antique & Collectible, Longest	$14.95

FURNITURE

1457	American **Oak** Furniture, McNerney	$9.95
3716	American **Oak** Furniture, Book II, McNerney	$12.95
1118	Antique **Oak** Furniture, Hill	$7.95
2271	Collector's Encyclopedia of **American** Furniture, Vol. II, Swedberg	$24.95
3720	Collector's Encyclopedia of **American** Furniture, Vol. III, Swedberg	$24.95
5359	Early **American** Furniture, Obbard	$12.95
1755	Furniture of the **Depression Era**, Swedberg	$19.95
3906	**Heywood-Wakefield** Modern Furniture, Rouland	$18.95
1885	**Victorian** Furniture, Our American Heritage, McNerney	$9.95

3829	**Victorian** Furniture, Our American Heritage, Book II, McNerney	$9.95

JEWELRY, HATPINS, WATCHES & PURSES

1712	Antique & Collectible **Thimbles** & Accessories, Mathis	$19.95
1748	Antique **Purses**, Revised Second Ed., Holiner	$19.95
1278	Art Nouveau & Art Deco **Jewelry**, Baker	$9.95
4850	Collectible **Costume Jewelry**, Simonds	$24.95
3722	Collector's Ency. of **Compacts**, Carryalls & Face Powder Boxes, Mueller	$24.95
4940	**Costume Jewelry**, A Practical Handbook & Value Guide, Rezazadeh	$24.95
1716	Fifty Years of Collectible **Fashion Jewelry**, 1925–1975, Baker	$19.95
1424	**Hatpins** & Hatpin Holders, Baker	$9.95
1181	100 Years of Collectible **Jewelry**, 1850–1950, Baker	$9.95
4729	**Sewing Tools** & Trinkets, Thompson	$24.95
5620	Unsigned Beauties of **Costume Jewelry**, Brown	$24.95
4878	Vintage & Contemporary **Purse Accessories**, Gerson	$24.95
3830	Vintage **Vanity Bags** & Purses, Gerson	$24.95

INDIANS, GUNS, KNIVES, TOOLS, PRIMITIVES

1868	Antique **Tools**, Our American Heritage, McNerney	$9.95
5616	Big Book of **Pocket Knives**, Stewart	$19.95
4943	Field Guide to Flint **Arrowheads** & Knives of the North American Indian	$9.95
3885	**Indian Artifacts** of the Midwest, Book II, Hothem	$16.95
4870	**Indian Artifacts** of the Midwest, Book III, Hothem	$18.95
5685	**Indian Artifacts** of the Midwest, Book IV, Hothem	$19.95
5687	**Modern Guns**, Identification & Values, 13th Ed., Quertermous	$14.95
2164	**Primitives**, Our American Heritage, McNerney	$9.95
1759	**Primitives**, Our American Heritage, 2nd Series, McNerney	$14.95
4730	Standard **Knife** Collector's Guide, 3rd Ed., Ritchie & Stewart	$12.95

PAPER COLLECTIBLES & BOOKS

4633	**Big Little Books**, Jacobs	$18.95
4710	Collector's Guide to **Children's Books**, 1850 to 1950, Jones	$18.95
5596	Collector's Guide to **Children's Books**, 1950 to 1975, Jones	$19.95
1441	Collector's Guide to **Post Cards**, Wood	$9.95
2081	Guide to Collecting **Cookbooks**, Allen	$14.95
5613	Huxford's **Old Book** Value Guide, 12th Ed.	$19.95
2080	Price Guide to **Cookbooks** & Recipe Leaflets, Dickinson	$9.95
3973	**Sheet Music** Reference & Price Guide, 2nd Ed., Pafik & Guiheen	$19.95
4654	**Victorian Trade Cards**, Historical Reference & Value Guide, Cheadle	$19.95
4733	**Whitman Juvenile Books**, Brown	$17.95

GLASSWARE

5602	Anchor Hocking's **Fire-King** & More, 2nd Ed.	$24.95
4561	Collectible **Drinking Glasses**, Chase & Kelly	$17.95
4642	Collectible **Glass Shoes**, Wheatley	$19.95
5357	Coll. **Glassware** from the 40s, 50s & 60s, 5th Ed., Florence	$19.95
1810	Collector's Encyclopedia of **American Art Glass**, Shuman	$29.95
5358	Collector's Encyclopedia of **Depression Glass**, 14th Ed., Florence	$19.95
1961	Collector's Encyclopedia of **Fry Glassware**, Fry Glass Society	$24.95
1664	Collector's Encyclopedia of **Heisey Glass**, 1925–1938, Bredehoft	$24.95
3905	Collector's Encyclopedia of **Milk Glass**, Newbound	$24.95
4936	Collector's Guide to **Candy Containers**, Dezso/Poirier	$19.95
4564	**Crackle Glass**, Weitman	$19.95
4941	**Crackle Glass**, Book II, Weitman	$19.95
4714	**Czechoslovakian Glass** and Collectibles, Book II, Barta/Rose	$16.95
5528	Early American **Pattern Glass**, Metz	$17.95
5682	**Elegant Glassware** of the Depression Era, 9th Ed., Florence	$19.95
5614	Field Guide to **Pattern Glass**, McCain	$17.95
3981	Evers' Standard **Cut Glass** Value Guide	$12.95
4659	**Fenton** Art Glass, 1907–1939, Whitmyer	$24.95
5615	Florence's **Glassware Pattern Identification** Guide, Vol. II	$19.95
3725	**Fostoria**, Pressed, Blown & Hand Molded Shapes, Kerr	$24.95
4719	**Fostoria**, Etched, Carved & Cut Designs, Vol. II, Kerr	$24.95

COLLECTOR BOOKS
Informing Today's Collector

3883	**Fostoria Stemware**, The Crystal for America, Long/Seate	$24.95
5261	**Fostoria Tableware**, 1924 – 1943, Long/Seate	$24.95
5361	**Fostoria Tableware**, 1944 – 1986, Long/Seate	$24.95
5604	**Fostoria**, Useful & Ornamental, Long/Seate	$29.95
4644	**Imperial Carnival Glass**, Burns	$18.95
3886	**Kitchen Glassware** of the Depression Years, 5th Ed., Florence	$19.95
5600	Much More Early American **Pattern Glass**, Metz	$17.95
5690	Pocket Guide to **Depression Glass**, 12th Ed., Florence	$9.95
5594	Standard Encyclopedia of **Carnival Glass**, 7th Ed., Edwards/Carwile	$29.95
5595	Standard **Carnival Glass** Price Guide, 12th Ed., Edwards/Carwile	$9.95
5272	Standard Encyclopedia of **Opalescent Glass**, 3rd Ed., Edwards/Carwile	$24.95
5617	Standard Encyclopedia of **Pressed Glass**, 2nd Ed., Edwards/Carwile	$29.95
4731	**Stemware Identification**, Featuring Cordials with Values, Florence	$24.95
4732	**Very Rare Glassware** of the Depression Years, 5th Series, Florence	$24.95
4656	**Westmoreland Glass**, Wilson	$24.95

POTTERY

4927	**ABC Plates & Mugs**, Lindsay	$24.95
4929	**American Art Pottery**, Sigafoose	$24.95
4630	**American Limoges**, Limoges	$24.95
1312	**Blue & White Stoneware**, McNerney	$9.95
1958	So. Potteries **Blue Ridge Dinnerware**, 3rd Ed., Newbound	$14.95
1959	**Blue Willow**, 2nd Ed., Gaston	$14.95
4851	Collectible **Cups & Saucers**, Harran	$18.95
1373	Collector's Encyclopedia of **American Dinnerware**, Cunningham	$24.95
4931	Collector's Encyclopedia of **Bauer Pottery**, Chipman	$24.95
4932	Collector's Encyclopedia of **Blue Ridge Dinnerware**, Vol. II, Newbound	$24.95
4658	Collector's Encyclopedia of **Brush-McCoy Pottery**, Huxford	$24.95
5034	Collector's Encyclopedia of **California Pottery**, 2nd Ed., Chipman	$24.95
2133	Collector's Encyclopedia of **Cookie Jars**, Roerig	$24.95
3723	Collector's Encyclopedia of **Cookie Jars**, Book II, Roerig	$24.95
4939	Collector's Encyclopedia of **Cookie Jars**, Book III, Roerig	$24.95
5040	Collector's Encyclopedia of **Fiesta**, 8th Ed., Huxford	$19.95
4718	Collector's Encyclopedia of **Figural Planters & Vases**, Newbound	$19.95
3961	Collector's Encyclopedia of **Early Noritake**, Alden	$24.95
1439	Collector's Encyclopedia of **Flow Blue China**, Gaston	$19.95
3812	Collector's Encyclopedia of **Flow Blue China**, 2nd Ed., Gaston	$24.95
3431	Collector's Encyclopedia of **Homer Laughlin China**, Jasper	$24.95
1276	Collector's Encyclopedia of **Hull Pottery**, Roberts	$19.95
3962	Collector's Encyclopedia of **Lefton China**, DeLozier	$19.95
4855	Collector's Encyclopedia of **Lefton China**, Book II, DeLozier	$19.95
5609	Collector's Encyclopedia of **Limoges Porcelain**, 3rd Ed., Gaston	$24.95
2334	Collector's Encyclopedia of **Majolica Pottery**, Katz-Marks	$19.95
1358	Collector's Encyclopedia of **McCoy Pottery**, Huxford	$19.95
3837	Collector's Encyclopedia of **Nippon Porcelain**, Van Patten	$24.95
2089	Collector's Ency. of **Nippon Porcelain**, 2nd Series, Van Patten	$24.95
1665	Collector's Ency. of **Nippon Porcelain**, 3rd Series, Van Patten	$24.95
4712	Collector's Ency. of **Nippon Porcelain**, 4th Series, Van Patten	$24.95
1447	Collector's Encyclopedia of **Noritake**, Van Patten	$19.95
1037	Collector's Encyclopedia of **Occupied Japan**, 1st Series, Florence	$14.95
1038	Collector's Encyclopedia of **Occupied Japan**, 2nd Series, Florence	$14.95
2335	Collector's Encyclopedia of **Occupied Japan**, 5th Series, Florence	$14.95
4951	Collector's Encyclopedia of **Old Ivory China**, Hillman	$24.95
5564	Collector's Encyclopedia of **Pickard China**, Reed	$29.95
3877	Collector's Encyclopedia of **R.S. Prussia**, 4th Series, Gaston	$24.95
5618	Collector's Encyclopedia of **Rosemeade Pottery**, Dommel	$24.95
1034	Collector's Encyclopedia of **Roseville Pottery**, Huxford	$19.95
1035	Collector's Encyclopedia of **Roseville Pottery**, 2nd Ed., Huxford	$19.95
4856	Collector's Encyclopedia of **Russel Wright**, 2nd Ed., Kerr	$24.95
4713	Collector's Encyclopedia of **Salt Glaze Stoneware**, Taylor/Lowrance	$24.95
3314	Collector's Encyclopedia of **Van Briggle Art Pottery**, Sasicki	$24.95
4563	Collector's Encyclopedia of **Wall Pockets**, Newbound	$19.95
2111	Collector's Encyclopedia of **Weller Pottery**, Huxford	$29.95
3876	Collector's Guide to **Lu-Ray Pastels**, Meehan	$18.95
3814	Collector's Guide to **Made in Japan Ceramics**, White	$18.95

4646	Collector's Guide to **Made in Japan Ceramics**, Book II, White	$18.95
2339	Collector's Guide to **Shawnee Pottery**, Vanderbilt	$19.95
1425	**Cookie Jars**, Westfall	$9.95
3440	**Cookie Jars**, Book II, Westfall	$19.95
4924	Figural & Novelty **Salt & Pepper Shakers**, 2nd Series, Davern	$24.95
2379	Lehner's Ency. of **U.S. Marks** on Pottery, Porcelain & China	$24.95
4722	**McCoy Pottery**, Collector's Reference & Value Guide, Hanson/Nissen	$19.95
1670	**Red Wing Collectibles**, DePasquale	$9.95
1440	**Red Wing Stoneware**, DePasquale	$9.95
1632	**Salt & Pepper Shakers**, Guarnaccia	$9.95
5091	**Salt & Pepper Shakers** II, Guarnaccia	$18.95
2220	**Salt & Pepper Shakers** III, Guarnaccia	$14.95
3443	**Salt & Pepper Shakers** IV, Guarnaccia	$18.95
3738	**Shawnee Pottery**, Mangus	$24.95
4629	Turn of the Century **American Dinnerware**, 1880s–1920s, Jasper	$24.95
3327	**Watt Pottery** – Identification & Value Guide, Morris	$19.95

OTHER COLLECTIBLES

4704	Antique & Collectible **Buttons**, Wisniewski	$19.95
2269	Antique **Brass & Copper** Collectibles, Gaston	$16.95
1880	Antique **Iron**, McNerney	$9.95
3872	Antique **Tins**, Dodge	$24.95
4845	Antique **Typewriters & Office Collectibles**, Rehr	$19.95
5607	Antiquing and Collecting on the **Internet**, Parry	$12.95
1128	**Bottle** Pricing Guide, 3rd Ed., Cleveland	$7.95
4636	**Celluloid** Collectibles, Dunn	$14.95
3718	Collectible **Aluminum**, Grist	$16.95
4560	Collectible **Cats**, An Identification & Value Guide, Book II, Fyke	$19.95
4852	Collectible **Compact Disc** Price Guide 2, Cooper	$17.95
5666	Collector's Encyclopedia of **Granite Ware**, Book 2, Greguire	$29.95
4705	Collector's Guide to **Antique Radios**, 4th Ed., Bunis	$18.95
5608	Collector's Gde. to Buying, Selling, & Trading on the **Internet**, 2nd Ed., Hix	$12.95
3880	Collector's Guide to **Cigarette Lighters**, Flanagan	$17.95
4637	Collector's Guide to **Cigarette Lighters**, Book II, Flanagan	$17.95
4942	Collector's Guide to **Don Winton Designs**, Ellis	$19.95
3966	Collector's Guide to **Inkwells**, Identification & Values, Badders	$18.95
4947	Collector's Guide to **Inkwells**, Book II, Badders	$19.95
5621	Collector's Guide to **Online Auctions**, Hix	$12.95
4862	Collector's Guide to **Toasters** & Accessories, Greguire	$19.95
4652	Collector's Guide to **Transistor Radios**, 2nd Ed., Bunis	$16.95
4864	Collector's Guide to **Wallace Nutting Pictures**, Ivankovich	$18.95
1629	**Doorstops**, Identification & Values, Bertoia	$9.95
4717	Figural **Nodders**, Includes Bobbin' Heads and Swayers, Irtz	$19.95
5683	**Fishing Lure** Collectibles, 2nd Ed., Murphy/Edmisten	$29.95
5259	**Flea Market Trader**, 12th Ed., Huxford	$9.95
4945	**G-Men and FBI Toys** and Collectibles, Whitworth	$18.95
5605	**Garage Sale & Flea Market Annual**, 8th Ed.	$19.95
3819	**General Store** Collectibles, Wilson	$24.95
5159	Huxford's Collectible **Advertising**, 4th Ed	$24.95
2216	**Kitchen Antiques**, 1790–1940, McNerney	$14.95
4950	The **Lone Ranger**, Collector's Reference & Value Guide, Felbinger	$18.95
2026	**Railroad** Collectibles, 4th Ed., Baker	$14.95
5619	**Roy Rogers and Dale Evans** Toys & Memorabilia, Coyle	$24.95
5367	**Schroeder's Antiques Price Guide**, 18th Ed., Huxford	$12.95
5007	**Silverplated Flatware**, Revised 4th Edition, Hagan	$18.95
1922	Standard **Old Bottle** Price Guide, Sellari	$14.95
5694	Summers' Guide to **Coca-Cola**, 3rd Ed.	$24.95
5356	Summers' Pocket Guide to **Coca-Cola**, 2nd Ed.	$9.95
3892	**Toy & Miniature Sewing Machines**, Thomas	$18.95
4876	**Toy & Miniature Sewing Machines**, Book II, Thomas	$24.95
5144	Value Guide to **Advertising Memorabilia**, 2nd Ed., Summers	$19.95
3977	Value Guide to **Gas Station Memorabilia**, Summers & Priddy	$24.95
4877	Vintage **Bar Ware**, Visakay	$24.95
4935	The W.F. Cody **Buffalo Bill** Collector's Guide with Values	$24.95
5281	**Wanted to Buy**, 7th Edition	$9.95

This is only a partial listing of the books on antiques that are available from Collector Books. All books are well illustrated and contain current values. Most of these books are available from your local bookseller, antique dealer, or public library. If you are unable to locate certain titles in your area, you may order by mail from COLLECTOR BOOKS, P.O. Box 3009, Paducah, KY 42002-3009. Customers with Visa, Discover or MasterCard may phone in orders from 7:00–5:00 CST, Monday–Friday, Toll Free 1-800-626-5420; www.collectorbooks.com. Add $3.00 for postage for the first book ordered and 50¢ for each additional book. Include item number, title, and price when ordering. Allow 14 to 21 days for delivery.

Schroeder's ANTIQUES Price Guide

OUR #1 BEST-SELLER!

...is the #1 bestselling antiques & collectibles value guide on the market today, and here's why...

• *More than 450 advisors, well-known dealers, and top-notch collectors work together with our editors to bring you accurate information regarding pricing and identification.*

• *More than 45,000 items in almost 500 categories are listed along with hundreds of sharp original photos that illustrate not only the rare and unusual, but the common, popular collectibles as well.*

• *Each large close-up shot shows important details clearly. Every subject is represented with histories and background information, a feature not found in any of our competitors' publications.*

• *Our editors keep abreast of newly developing trends, often adding several new categories a year as the need arises.*

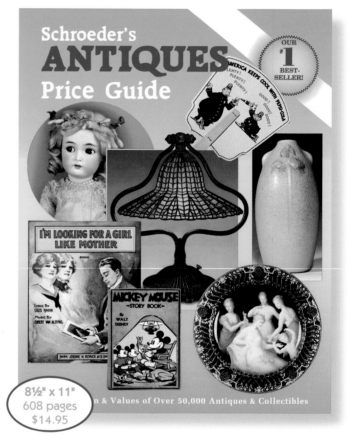

Schroeder's ANTIQUES Price Guide

OUR #1 BEST-SELLER!

8½" x 11"
608 pages
$14.95

Identification & Values of Over 50,000 Antiques & Collectibles

If it merits the interest of today's collector, you'll find it in *Schroeder's*. And you can feel confident that the information we publish is up-to-date and accurate. Our advisors thoroughly check each category to spot inconsistencies, listings that may not be entirely reflective of market dealings, and lines too vague to be of merit. Only the best of the lot remains for publication.

cb
COLLECTOR BOOKS
A Division of Schroeder Publishing Co., Inc.

Without doubt, you'll find
Schroeder's Antiques Price Guide
the only one to buy for
reliable information and values.

COLLECTOR BOOKS
P.O. Box 3009 • Paducah, KY 42002–3009
www.collectorbooks.com